SEASONS OF PRAYER: In Word and Image

ISBN 1-56292-541-5

Copyright © 1999 by Dr. Kenneth Boa

Photography by Carl Alan Smith

Published by Honor Books

P.O. Box 55388

Tulsa, Oklahoma 74155

Design by David Uttley Design

*This book is affectionately dedicated
to the members of the Reflections Ministries team:*

Karen Boa, Heather Cottingham, George Grove,
Barry Morrow, Aseervadam Rampogu, Len Sykes,
Al Van Home, Lochraine Wall, Archie Wanamaker,
and to the memory of Edward G. Dudley, Jr.,
a beloved Reflections team member who has
entered into the joy of his Master.

DR. KENNETH BOA

I would like to thank . . .

Joe Kenner, Florida naturalist and friend,
who shared his visions and love of the great outdoors with me.

Galen Rowell, whose teaching and writings
inspired me to realize that you really can be passionate about bringing back images
that capture what you saw and felt.

Eve Smith who gave me
a camera in 1988 and encouraged me to go out and use it.

Charlie Jarman, who came up from
the low country to show me how to shoot my own native mountains.

My parents, who took me outdoors almost
every weekend as a child to the farms, mountains, streams, and ponds
around my hometown in North Georgia.

CARL ALAN SMITH

Table of Contents

Dr. Kenneth Boa

I have delighted and reveled in the beauty of nature for as long as I can remember. As a boy, I spent a great deal of time in wooded areas, pastures, streams, and gardens discovering endless pleasure in jack-in-the-pulpits, ladybugs, fireflies, sunflowers, gardenias, hydrangeas, tadpoles, butterflies, sassafras roots, birch trees, pear trees, leaves, rocks, minerals, clouds, sunsets, snowflakes, and a thousand other joys.

For some reason, this childlike sense of wonder and awe at the natural order still remains with me. The more I learn, the more mysterious everything continues to become, and the less I take for granted. For me, nature always points beyond itself. The subtlety, complexity, variety, intricacy, and beauty of the created order speaks eloquently of the marvels and mystery of the One Who designed it and spoke it into being.

God reveals Himself in the world of nature and also in the Scripture. When my wife Karen and I created Simple Prayers, we described it as "a tool that combines the Word of the Lord with prayer and guides you through the process of praying Scripture back to God." It will enable you to think God's thoughts after Him and to personalize them in your own thinking and practice. Because it is based on Scripture, you can be assured that these prayers will be pleasing to God. This book will encourage you in your walk with God by enriching and enhancing the quality of your experience of prayer.

It occurred to me that it would be particularly effective to combine the world (God's general revelation) and the Word (God's special revelation) in such a way that each would reinforce the other. A few years ago, I met Carl Alan Smith, and I have admired his skillful and captivating photography ever since. Carl enthusiastically responded to my vision of combining his photography with some of the Scripture selections in Simple Prayers, creating a book of evident beauty and quality. *Seasons of Prayer: In Word and Image* is the product of this vision, and it is my hope that many of its users will take the time to reflect upon the biblical passages while enjoying the photographs. The time you invest in this process will enhance your appreciation of both the creation and the Creator.

Kenneth D. Boa

Carl Alan Smith

Providing images to accompany meditation, prayers, or music can sometimes diminish the experience of communing with your own imagination. I remember how much I disliked the idea of music videos after years of conjuring my own images to go with popular songs. With so many days of our lives overwhelmed by the daily grind and frantic blitz of media, the simple beauty of the natural world around us can be lost.

Whether it is in one of the earth's spectacular places or in our own backyard, it is the privilege and challenge of the photographer to tune into these visual gifts and remind us of those special and rare moments that dwell in our common memory.

Galen Rowell often says that the successful photographer must capture a moment that matches the very best of our memory of a place or time. If we see a photograph of an entire lake where we spent a wonderful weekend, and that image was taken at high noon in hazy light, it won't bring back the special feelings that we had when we walked up to our red canoe in the early morning mist. The photograph should capture the feeling of that experience without having to say, "You had to be there."

When Ken Boa first saw my photos and expressed an interest in including them in this book, we discussed the need for quality images that would stand alone and meet the criteria that Galen describes. Ken was kind enough to think my work worthy of this simple test—I sincerely hope you agree.

I only know for sure that searching for these special moments has become a wonderful passion and has allowed me to become lost in time while connecting with this amazing planet in a purposeful way. If even one image here brings to mind a favorite memory or evokes a desire to experience a place you've never seen, I have succeeded.

Birth, growth, decay, death; spring, summer, fall, winter—the seasons of our lives correspond to the seasons of each year. Each day is also a "mini-life," an entity unto itself. As a new day dawns, we arise from the mysterious deathlike state we describe as sleep.

Some of us are up well before sunrise, and others long afterward; "morning people" are soon ready for action, while the rest of us move through a gradual process of becoming fully awake, increasingly "alive" to the possibilities and challenges of the day.

Somewhere along the way, we reach the peak of our energies and productivity, and then we begin to decline. We may get a "second wind," but fatigue gradually sets in as the "fall" of our day turns to "winter."

As the day ends for us, whether at 9:30 p.m. or 1:30 a.m., we put on our night clothes, turn out the lights, get into bed, and in the darkness pull our "shrouds" over our bodies. Slowly but surely, we sink into the oblivion of slumber. Hours later, the sun rises, and we emerge once again from our cocoon-like state. We have been "resurrected" into another day, and another "mini-life" is ready to run its course.

Scripture calls us to live one day at a time without worrying about tomorrow or reliving the past. The Lord tells us to be alive to the now, and to live in the precious present, especially in view of the brevity of our earthly sojourn. Consider this imagery from Ephesians 5:14 NAS:

Awake, sleeper,

And arise from the dead,

And Christ will shine on you.

Winter is a reminder of the "way of all flesh," but it also anticipates the reality and incomprehensible wonder of the resurrection. The dormant state of hibernating animals and of barren trees under shrouds of snow, the coldness of the air, and the clarity of the night sky with its icy starlight—all of these are vehicles of beauty and promise. Winter is the womb of the manifold births of spring.

I will not fear, for You are with me;

I will not be dismayed, for You are my God.

You will strengthen me and help me;

You will uphold me with Your righteous right hand.

For You are the Lord my God,

who takes hold of my right hand

And says to me, "Do not fear; I will help you."

ISAIAH 41:10, 13

This poor man cried out,

and the Lord heard him,

And saved him out of all his troubles.

The angel of the Lord encamps around

those who fear Him,

And delivers them.

PSALM 34:6-7

I waited patiently for the Lord,

And He turned to me and heard my cry.

God lifted me out of the slimy pit,

out of the mud and mire;

He set my feet on a rock and

gave me a firm place to stand.

He put a new song in my mouth,

a hymn of praise to our God.

Many will see and fear

And put their trust in the Lord.

PSALM 40:1-3

All Your works will praise You, O Lord,

And Your saints will bless You.

They will speak of the glory of Your kingdom

And talk of Your power,

So that all men may know of Your mighty acts

And the glorious majesty of Your kingdom.

Your kingdom is an everlasting kingdom,

And Your dominion endures through all generations.

PSALM 145:10-13

The Lord is great and greatly to be praised;

He is to be feared above all gods.

For all the gods of the nations are idols,

But the Lord made the heavens.

Splendor and majesty are before Him;

Strength and joy are in His place.

I will ascribe to the Lord glory and strength.

I will ascribe to the Lord the glory due His name

And worship the Lord in the beauty of holiness.

Tremble before him, all the earth.

The world is firmly established, it will not be moved.

1 CHRONICLES 16:25-30

Who

Who is like You, O Lord?
Who is like You—majestic in holiness,
Awesome in praises, working wonders?

EXODUS 15:11

There is no one holy like the Lord;

There is no one besides You;

Nor is there any Rock like our God.

1 SAMUEL 2:2

How great are Your works, O Lord!

Your thoughts are very deep.

The senseless man does not know;

Fools do not understand

That when the wicked spring up like grass

And all the evildoers flourish,

They will be destroyed forever.

But You, O Lord, are exalted forever.

PSALM 92:5-8

THE LORD BLESS YOU AND KEEP YOU; THE LORD MAKE HIS FACE SHINE UPON YOU AND BE GRACIOUS

TO YOU; THE LORD TURN HIS FACE TOWARD YOU AND GIVE YOU PEACE. NUMBERS 6:24-26

The Lord will command His lovingkindness by day,

And His song will be in the night—

A prayer to the God of my life.

PSALM 42:8

Blessed be the Lord God, the God of Israel,

Who alone does wonderful things.

And blessed be His glorious name forever;

May the whole earth be filled with His glory.

Amen and Amen.

PSALM 72:18-19

"Come now, let us reason together," says the Lord.

"Though your sins are like scarlet,

they shall be white as snow;

though they are red as crimson,

they shall be like wool."

ISAIAH 1:18

Long-awaited spring, especially in northern climates, never fails to satisfy the long-ings prompted by the sluggishness, cold, and relative barrenness of winter. Nature, awakening from a trance, once again brings an awesome panorama of buds, flowers, colors, and fragrances as the year moves into its adolescence. The soulful blending of bird calls, the gentle and sweet-smelling breezes, and the variegated colors of blossoming trees enrapture the senses of those who are attuned to such wonders.

Each day holds new surprises, yet few of us pause long enough to notice them and delight in them. Somehow, "Nice day, isn't it?" fails to capture the living and burgeoning marvels that surround us.

I have a "nature kit." Among other things, it includes a set of field lenses that range from five to twenty magnifications and a high-intensity battery-powered miniature light. From time to time, especially when I visit the countryside, I use my nature kit to peer into flowers, leaves, and insects to see the miniature structures, patterns, and colors that are invisible to the unaided eye. For me, this is an act of worship.

Martin Luther once held a rose in his hand and said, "Tis a magnificent work of God: could a man make but one such rose as this, he would be thought worthy of all honor, but the gifts of God lose their value in our eyes, from their very infinity."

Consider a flower with its subtle interwoven colors, its exquisite structure, its lovely fragrance, its symmetry, its texture, its evident design and variegated functions—and realize that all of this springs from the dirt! Then contemplate the One Who created them by the trillions. I believe we honor the Lord when we take pleasure in the works of His hands.

And the Spring arose on the garden fair,
Like the Spirit of Love felt everywhere;
And each flower and herb on Earth's dark breast
Rose from the dreams of its wintry rest.
The snowdrop and then the violet,
Arose from the ground with warm rain wet;
And their breath was mixed with sweet odour sent
From the turf like the voice and the instrument.

—SHELLEY

I call this to mind, and therefore I have hope:

The Lord's mercies never cease,

for His compassions never fail.

They are new every morning; great is Your faithfulness.

SEASONS 32 OF PRAYER

The Lord Most High is awesome,

The great King over all the earth!

God is the King of all the earth,

And I will sing His praise.

God reigns over the nations;

God is seated on His holy throne.

PSALM 47:2, 7-8

You must be treated as holy by those who come near You,

and before all people, You will be honored.

LEVITICUS 10:3

Shout for joy, O heavens! Rejoice, O earth!

Break out into singing, O mountains!

For the Lord has comforted His people

And will have compassion on His afflicted.

ISAIAH 49:13

I will greatly rejoice in the Lord;

My soul will be joyful in my God.

For He has clothed me with garments of salvation

And arrayed me in a robe of righteousness,

As a bridegroom decks himself with ornaments,

And as a bride adorns herself with her jewels.

ISAIAH 61:10

O come, let us sing to the Lord;

Let us shout joyfully to the Rock of our salvation.

Let us come before His presence with thanksgiving;

Let us shout for joy to Him with psalms.

PSALM 95:1-2

O sing to the Lord a new song;

Sing to the Lord, all the earth.

Sing to the Lord, bless His name;

Proclaim the good news of His salvation day after day.

Declare His glory among the nations,

His marvelous works among all people.

PSALM 96:1-3

Are You a God nearby,

And not a God far away?

Can anyone hide in secret places

So that You cannot see him?

Do You not fill heaven and earth?

JEREMIAH 23:23-24

Let the words of my mouth and the meditation of my heart
Be pleasing in Your sight,
O Lord, my Rock and my Redeemer.

PSALM 19:14

Thus says the Lord: "Let not the wise man boast of his wisdom, and let not the strong man boast of his strength, and let not the rich man boast of his riches; but let him who boasts boast about this: that he understands and knows Me, that I am the Lord, who exercises lovingkindness, justice, and righteousness on earth; for in these I delight," declares the Lord.   JEREMIAH 9:23-24

Where were you when I laid the foundations of the earth?

Tell Me, if you have understanding.

Who determined its measurements?

Surely you know!

Or who stretched the line across it?

On what were its bases sunk,

Or who laid its cornerstone,

When the morning stars sang together

And all the sons of God shouted for joy?

JOB 38:4-7

You formed my inward parts;

You wove me together in my mother's womb.

I thank You because I am fearfully and wonderfully made;

Your works are wonderful, and my soul knows it full well.

My frame was not hidden from You

When I was made in secret

And skillfully wrought in the depths of the earth.

Your eyes saw my embryo, and all the days ordained for me

Were written in Your book

Before one of them came to be.

PSALM 139:13-16

Blessed is the man who finds wisdom,

And the man who gains understanding,

For its profit is greater than that of silver,

And its gain than fine gold.

She is more precious than jewels,

And nothing I desire can compare with her.

Long life is in her right hand;

In her left hand are riches and honor.

Her ways are pleasant ways,

And all her paths are peace.

She is a tree of life to those who embrace her,

And happy are those who hold her fast.

PROVERBS 3:13-18

As the year reaches the peak of its abundance, the natural order becomes extravagant in its diversity.

When our family lived in England, summer was easily our favorite season. During those months, I occasionally went off by myself on country walks, and these were always rich times of reflection and renewal. Karen and I often took drives from Oxford into the country, and we especially loved the magnificent gardens such as those at Sissinghurst Castle, Hidcote Manor, Wisley Gardens, Nymans, Oxford Botanic Garden, and the Royal Botanic Gardens at Kew.

Gardens illustrate several spiritual truths. They are divine-human products—the design and life of the plants is derived from God, but the placement and nurturing of the plants depends on human choices. Gardens point to the reality of both divine sovereignty and human responsibility. We may plan, plant, cultivate, water, and fertilize the plants, but in the end, we can no more make the plants come out of the soil than we can add a decade to our lifespan. Gardening requires dependence, patience, and consistency.

MMER

Gardens also speak of unity in diversity. A well-planned garden is not a random or chaotic affair, but results from a comprehensive design that juxtaposes plants in ways that account for color, species, shape and size, light requirements, and aesthetic appeal. Each plant in a great garden contributes to the larger whole, just as each unique member in the body of Christ contributes something of value and significance.

Gardens are also subject to attacks by brutal and fickle weather conditions, as well as pests and diseases. And they involve pruning, some plants requiring more than others. Karen has many rose bushes, and I dislike watching her prune them, since some need such severe measures that I keep thinking they will not survive. The summer always proves me wrong as I see her roses flourishing.

Any garden, left to itself, will become overgrown with weeds. Vigilance and regular maintenance are prerequisites to a beautiful and abundant garden. So it is with our inner, spiritual gardens. Dependence, discipline, planning, weeding, cultivation, watering, fertilization, pruning, and vigilance against attacks are all part of the growing and flourishing spiritual life.

I am convinced that neither death nor life,

nor angels nor principalities, nor things present nor things to come,

nor powers, nor height nor depth,

nor anything else in all creation,

will be able to separate me

from the love of God that is in Christ Jesus my Lord.

ROMANS 8:38-39

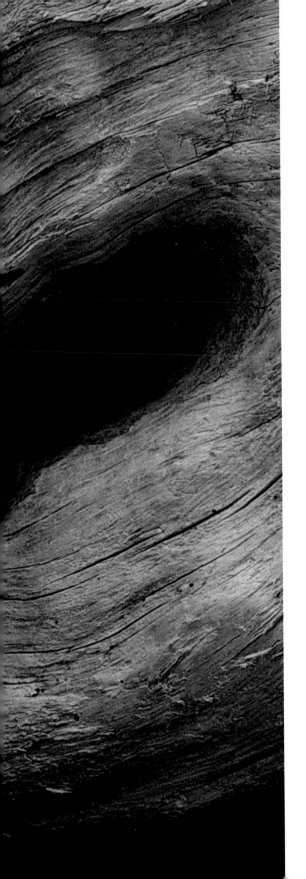

O Lord, You have searched me and You know me.

You know when I sit down and when I rise up;

You understand my thoughts from afar.

You scrutinize my path and my lying down

And are acquainted with all my ways.

Before a word is on my tongue,

O Lord, You know it completely.

You have enclosed me behind and before,

And laid Your hand upon me.

Such knowledge is too wonderful for me;

It is too lofty for me to attain.

PSALM 139:1-6

Bless the Lord, O my soul;

And all that is within me, bless His holy name.

Bless the Lord, O my soul,

And forget not all His benefits;

Who forgives all your iniquities

And heals all your diseases;

Who redeems your life from the pit

And crowns you with love and compassion;

Who satisfies your desires with good things,

So that your youth is renewed like the eagle's.

PSALM 103:1-5

Great and marvelous are Your works,
Lord God Almighty!
Righteous and true are Your ways,
King of the nations!
Who will not fear You, O Lord, and glorify Your name?
For You alone are holy.
All nations will come and worship before You,
For Your righteous acts have been revealed.

REVELATION 15:3-4

Hallelujah! Salvation and glory and power belong to our God,
because His judgments are true and righteous.

Oh, the depth of the riches both of the wisdom
and knowledge of God! How unsearchable are
Your judgments, and Your ways past finding out!
For who has known the mind of the Lord?
Or who has been Your counselor?
Or who has first given to You,
That You should repay him?
For from You and through You and to You are all
things. To You be the glory forever! Amen.

ROMANS 11:33-36

SEASONS 60 OF PRAYER

"The Lord is my portion," says my soul,
"Therefore I will wait for Him."
The Lord is good to those who wait for Him,
To the soul who seeks Him.
It is good to hope silently for the salvation of the Lord.

LAMENTATIONS 3:24-26

The Son of Man will come with the clouds of heaven. In the presence of the Ancient of Days, He will be given dominion and glory and a kingdom, so that all peoples, nations, and men of every language will worship Him. His dominion is an everlasting dominion that will not pass away, and His kingdom is one that will never be destroyed.   DANIEL 7:13-14

Who shall separate me from the love of Christ?

Shall tribulation, or distress, or persecution, or famine,

or nakedness, or danger, or sword?

As it is written:

"For Your sake we face death all day long;

We are considered as sheep to be slaughtered."

Yet in all these things I am more than a conqueror

through Him who loved me.

ROMANS 8:35-37

How precious are Your thoughts to me, O God!

How vast is the sum of them!

If I should count them, they would outnumber the grains of sand.

When I awake, I am still with You.

PSALM 139:17-18

To whom can I liken You or count You equal?

To whom can I compare You that You may be alike?

ISAIAH 46:5

I will enter Your gates with thanksgiving

And Your courts with praise;

I will give thanks to You and bless Your name.

For the Lord is good

And Your lovingkindness endures forever;

Your faithfulness continues through all generations.

PSALM 100:4-5

May the glory of the Lord endure forever;

May the Lord rejoice in His works.

PSALM 104:31

When I was in grammar school in northern New Jersey, my favorite school project in first and second grades was creating an album collection of colorful fall leaves. There was such an abundance and diversity of deciduous trees in our area that this was easy to do, and I vividly recall the pleasure I took in finding samples that would illustrate the variegated shapes and colors of the autumn foliage.

After culling out the leaves that didn't "make the cut," I brought my collection into the kitchen where my mother heated blocks of paraffin in a pan so that I could dip and seal each leaf before pasting it into my album. I would give a great deal to see one of those albums once again.

Like so many people, Karen and I love to drive into the mountains to see the fall colors. After a speaking engagement in Canada a few years ago, we spent a week together in a cottage on one of the Muskoka Lakes in Ontario. We timed this trip so that we would be there during the peak leaf season, and we were not disappointed. During our leisurely drives around the lakes and up into Algonquin Provincial Park, we enjoyed the most brilliant fall colors we have ever seen — an extraordinary composite of blazing reds, oranges, yellows, and purples, forming a visual cornucopia.

The true color inside the leaf comes out when the chlorophyll, the green pigment that is essential to the leaves' production of carbohydrates by photosynthesis, begins to disappear. Some trees that appear ordinary during the summer become glorious, while others merely turn brown.

Analogously, some people live quiet lives of trust and obedience and appear quite ordinary until late in their earthly sojourn. But in the end their true color emerges, and I have seen some of these faithful men and women of God go to their coronation in a blaze of glory. There are others who appeared impressive by the world's standards but whose end was marked by bitterness and emptiness, because they had fixed their hope on temporal things rather than the person of Christ. For me, the glory of autumn is an intimation of a coming glory that will never fade.

There is a time for everything,

and a season for every activity

under Heaven.

ECCLESIASTES 3:1

Blessed be the name of God for ever and ever,

For wisdom and power belong to Him.

He changes the times and the seasons;

He raises up kings and deposes them.

He gives wisdom to the wise

And knowledge to those who have understanding.

He reveals deep and hidden things;

He knows what is in the darkness,

And light dwells with Him.

DANIEL 2:20-22

How great You are, O Sovereign Lord!
There is no one like You, and there is no God besides You,
according to all that I have heard with my ears.

2 SAMUEL 7:22, 1 CHRONICLES 17:20

I know that You alone,
whose name is the Lord,
Are the Most High over all the earth.

O Lord, God of Israel, there is no God like You in

heaven above or on earth below;

You keep Your covenant and mercy with Your servants

who walk before You with all their heart.

1 KINGS 8:23, 2 CHRONICLES 6:14

I will exalt You, my God and King;

I will bless Your name for ever and ever.

Every day I will bless You,

And I will praise Your name for ever and ever.

Great is the Lord and most worthy of praise;

His greatness is unsearchable.

PSALM 145:1-3

Great is the Lord and most worthy of praise;

He is to be feared above all gods.

For all the gods of the nations are idols,

But the Lord made the heavens.

Splendor and majesty are before Him;

Strength and beauty are in His sanctuary.

I will ascribe to the Lord glory and strength.

I will ascribe to the Lord the glory due His name

And worship the Lord in the beauty of holiness.

PSALM 96:4-9

I am unworthy of all the lovingkindness and faithfulness
You have shown Your servant.

GENESIS 32:10

You are the God who answered me in the day of my
distress and have been with me wherever I have gone.

GENESIS 35:3

The Almighty is my shepherd,
the Rock of Israel,
who helps me and blesses me with
blessings of the heavens above.

GENESIS 49:24-25

God has made everything beautiful in its time.

He has also set eternity in the hearts of men;

yet they cannot fathom

what God has done from beginning to end.

ECCLESIASTES 3:11

PAGE 12 A simple fence in the snow. Shot one morning in the Colorado Rockies near mount Crested Butte on the road north toward Aspen.

 PAGE 15 A close-up of the summer growth on the Alaskan tundra, where tiny plants must bear their foliage and berries very quickly.

 PAGE 16 Morning light and fresh tracks in the snow combine to give both a warm and a chilly feel to this winter scene near Almont, Colorado.

 PAGE 19 The snow and ice of thousands of winters fills the valleys of the ice field around Mount Iliamma, Alaska. The drainage of such huge ice fields are glaciers "rivers of ice" which carve valleys and create new land forms.

 PAGE 20 Sunrise over Lake Iliamma, Alaska.

 PAGE 23 Ice storm along the Appalachian Trail near Nell's Gap, Georgia. Each season brings its own unique personality to the scenery.

 PAGE 24 Winter sunset in the Colorado Rockies near Almont.

 PAGE 27 Afternoon skies over a snow-covered hillside near Crested Butte, Colorado.

 PAGE 28 A detail of the ice on Exit Glacier, near Seward, Alaska. This ice is near the toe of the retreating glacier, and will soon melt after thousands of years of crawling along at inches per century in its frozen form.

 PAGE 33 A summer storm leaves its evidence on a Cleome blossom in the northern Georgia mountains. It rained out our picnic, but left a nice visual memory.

 PAGE 34 The setting sunlight hitting the face of Half Dome, the most distinctive formation in Yosemite National Park in California. The Merced River in the foreground traces the floor of Yosemite Valley where a glacier cut through solid rock millions of years ago.

 PAGE 36 The white trunks of young Aspen trees on Boulder Mountain in Utah. Below this grove of trees, in the hotter terrain, lies the barren beauty of Capitol Reef National Park, one of our least known western parks.

PAGE 39 Vernal Falls in Yosemite National Park, California. Melting snows after an unusually cold winter caused the falls to run at full force during this particular Spring.

 PAGE 40 Wildflowers along the marsh causeway leading to Sea Island, Georgia, from St. Simon's Island. The cabbage palms, salt-water marshes, wide beaches, and ocean surf give this part of the world its famous "low country" atmosphere.

 PAGE 42 Mist enshrouds the distant Monterey Cypress trees as they grow above the rocky banks of the shore on Montery Bay, California.

 PAGE 43 Flowers in a garden in the mountains of North Carolina. After traveling for miles through dramatic scenery, I shot this at the doorstep of my lodging. As far as I know, this was the shot that survived as the best of the day.

 PAGE 45 August Fireweed and mountains near Portage, Alaska, in route back from Seward.

 PAGE 46 The Hoh rain forest on the western mountain slopes of the Olympic National Park in Washington. Perhaps the wettest spot in the mainland United States. Almost every surface is coated with thick, wet moss.

 PAGE 49 A dew covered spider web on a cool northern Georgia morning. No need to travel to some far-off exotic location to find intimate, yet fleeting, beauty here.

 PAGE 53 When life gives you lemons . . . make lemonade. An overcast and foggy sky condition high in the mountains of North Carolina forced me to tune in the camera to the color and patterns at hand; in this case, the beauty of a flower blossom in the garden.

 PAGE 54 A solitary Alaskan wildflower finds refuge on a rocky riverbank next to a driftwood log. The dramatic scenery surrounding this image included the Pacific Ocean, a white water river crashing with chunks of ice the size of automobiles, several glaciers, and snow covered mountains

 PAGE 57 Once again, a cloudy foggy morning sent me to my knees to look at the little world immediately at my feet in a northern Georgia garden. The flower is long gone with its season, but its image remains because I was there to appreciate it for one brief moment.

PAGE 58 Yosemite Falls cascading into the valley floor in Yosemite National Park, California. The spring snowmelt creates a huge billow of water, which will dry to a trickle by the end of each summer.

 PAGE 61 Mono Lake's sea blue waters seem out of place in the baking desert country that surrounds it near the Nevada-California line. Miners and Mark Twain roamed and settled in the surrounding hills over a century ago when dreams of instant wealth temporarily turned deserts into boomtowns.

 PAGE 62 The afternoon sun hits the rapids of a rushing stream in the Sierra Mountains of California. The surrounding scenery was all grand, but this image, transfixing only one slice, captures the spirit of this particular place at this moment in time.

 PAGE 63 A sunset over the Rockies near Salt Lake City, Utah. I was standing at the mouth of Little Cottonwood Canyon shooting a small peak toward the east when my companion suggested I look back to the west. Good suggestion.

 PAGE 64 A clearing summer storm over the western scenery in Monument Valley on the Arizona-Utah border. This scene has been used a thousand times in western movies, but John Wayne wasn't there when I saw this double rainbow. I had given up on getting any good shots on such a gloomy day when I saw a break in the clouds at the horizon and ventured back to try my luck one more time.

 PAGE 66 The incoming tide on a rocky beach in Alaska near Katmai National Park. This beach was so remote it could only be reached by plane or boat far off the beaten path.

 PAGE 69 Backlit trees along the banks of the Merced River in Yosemite Valley, California. The fresh spring colors seem to glow from within when the morning light comes through them.

 PAGE 73 A Sweet Gum leaf in its autumn glory lies alone on a riverbank rock in the mountains of North Carolina.

 PAGE 74 Sunset after a storm from the Glacier Point overlook in Yosemite National Park. The flowing clouds seem to kiss the smooth weathered stone mountaintops.

PAGE 76 Simple grass blades and a sparkle of sun in a north Georgia farm pond. The camera can capture a moment of beauty so fleeting that your senses may enjoy it before your literal eye can register it.

 PAGE 77 Sunrise over Lake Iliamna, Alaska. Later that day I caught my first-ever Salmon. This shot caused me to miss a hot breakfast and rush to our plane, but as I look at this image, I never regret missing that meal.

 PAGE 79 Autumn mist in northern Georgia. On the right day, in the right light, even an ordinary little patch of woods can be magic. This was shot on a weekend ride near home with no particular mission to even take a photo.

 PAGE 80 Ducks on a lake in the Canadian Rockies. The weather was suited only for ducks and photographers.

 PAGE 83 Morning sunlight creating "Godbeams" through the mist around live oak trees on the isolated Cumberland Island, Georgia.

PAGE 84 The forest floor near my backyard in Atlanta caught my eye one fall afternoon after a rain with its endless patterns of subtle color.

Final Note:

Mr. Smith uses the Minolta Maxxum Series 35mm camera and lens system. Most of the photographs were taken with Fugichrome Velvia 50 ISO film and were shot with a camera mounted on a Slik Tripod with a pistol grip head or a Gitzo Mountaineer tripod. He also sometimes uses a polarizer filter, a graduated neutral density filter, or an 81 series warming filter. No filters are utilized which change the colors or otherwise distort the natural image.

KENNETH BOA is engaged in a ministry of relational evangelism and discipleship, teaching, writing, and speaking. He holds a B.S. from Case Institute of Technology, a Th.M. From Dallas Theological Seminary, a Ph.D. from New York University, and a D.Phil. from the University of Oxford in England.

Dr. Boa is the president of Reflections Ministries, an organization that seeks to provide safe places for people to consider the claims of Christ and to help them mature and bear fruit in their relationship with Him. He is also president of Trinity House Publishers, a publishing company that is dedicated to the creation of tools that will help people manifest eternal values in a temporal arena by drawing them to intimacy with God and a better understanding of the culture in which they live.

The author's publications include *Cults, World Religions, and the Occult; I'm Glad You Asked; Talk Thru the Bible; Visual Survey of the Bible; Drawing Near; Unraveling the Big Questions about God; Night Light; Handbook to Prayer; Handbook to Renewal; Simple Prayers; Face to Face* (two volumes); *An Unchanging Faith in a Changing World; and That I May Know Him.* He is a contributing editor to The Open Bible, the Promise Keeper's Men's Study Bible, The Leadership Bible, and the sole contributor to the Two-Year Daily Reading & Prayer Bible.

The author also writes a free monthly teaching letter called "Reflections." If you would like to be on the mailing list, call (800) DRAW NEAR (372-9632).

CARL ALAN SMITH discovered his passion for photography in 1989 on a trip to South America with the famous photographer Galen Rowell. Since then, he has taken his camera to most of the United States, including Alaska and Hawaii, as well as Canada, England, and the Caribbean.

A native Georgian, Smith practices architecture in Atlanta where he has resided since graduating from Georgia Tech in 1970. He has found photography to be the ideal vehicle to combine his love of travel and the outdoors with his professional artistic training as an architect.

"Before photography," Smith says, "I basically viewed my world as four seasons, two kinds of weather (rain or sun), and two kinds of scenery (beautiful and mundane). Seeing the world through my camera has awakened me to the infinite variety of beauty and its subtle changes from moment to moment, day to day, not just season to season. It has allowed me to appreciate and rejoice in the drama of a spiderweb in my backyard, as much as a sunset over the Sierras."

Smith's work has been published extensively in Germany and has been used for posters, guidebooks, coffee table books, post cards, and calendars in Europe and the United States.

He is represented in the United States by the Aristock agency.